Raising Lions:
The Art of Nurturing Confident and Courageous Children.

Maria Russell

TABLE OF CONTENT

Parenting for Confidence and Courage: A Summary and Reflection.

Introduction

Raising Lions: The Art of Nurturing Confident and Courageous Children is a must-read for any parent or caregiver seeking to encourage and empower their children. Written by Maria Russell an expert in the field of child development, this book offers a wealth of practical advice and insights on how to nurture confidence and courage in children of all ages.

Throughout the book, you'll find valuable tips and strategies for supporting your child's natural strengths and helping them build self-esteem and resilience. You'll learn how to set boundaries and establish clear expectations, as well as how to encourage your child to take on new challenges and learn from their mistakes.

In addition to providing practical guidance, Raising Lions also delves into the emotional and psychological aspects of raising confident and courageous children. You'll discover how to cultivate a positive and supportive home environment, as well as how to model the behaviors and attitudes you want your child to embody.

Whether you're a first-time parent or a seasoned caregiver, Raising Lions is an invaluable resource that will help you raise confident, courageous children who are ready to take on the world.

As parents, we all want to raise strong, independent, and resilient children who are capable of facing life's challenges with courage and determination. But how do we do this? How do we nurture the qualities that will help our children grow into confident and courageous adults?

In this book, we will explore the key principles and strategies for raising confident and courageous children. From setting clear boundaries and expectations, to encouraging a growth mindset and fostering a sense of purpose, we will provide practical tips and techniques that you can use to help your child develop the skills and qualities needed to thrive in today's world.

Whether you are a seasoned parent looking for new ideas, or a new parent seeking guidance and support, Raising Lions is an essential resource that will help you navigate the journey of parenting with confidence and grace."

CHAPTER 1

The Importance of Confidence and Courage in Child Development.

Confidence and courage are essential qualities for children to develop as they grow and navigate the challenges of life. Without these qualities, children may struggle with self-doubt, fear, and a lack of resilience, which can hold them back from reaching their full potential.

Confidence is an important foundation for children to build upon as they grow and develop. It helps children feel self-assured and capable, and enables them to take on new challenges and tasks with a sense of belief in their own abilities. When children feel confident, they are more likely to try new things, express themselves freely, and take risks that will help them learn and grow.

Similarly, courage is an important quality that allows children to overcome their fears and face challenges head-on. It gives children the strength and determination to stand up for what they believe in, and to pursue their goals and dreams despite any obstacles that may come their way. When children are courageous, they are more likely to persevere in the face of adversity and to take risks that will help them learn and grow.

It is commonly thought that educating a child means teaching him to respect the rules and filling him with the values of his own family, culture and society. Even educational institutions are often oriented towards introducing knowledge, skills, competences and learning into the child. The child is seen as an empty container to be filled .

But is it really so? We advocate the importance of autonomy so much and then at the same time we ask the child to be autonomous, but to do the things that we adults decide . This model of education has its roots in behavioral psychology where, according to the experiments of Ivan P. Pavlov (1903), a positive reinforcement (food) was given to the mouse to make it make certain choices and a negative reinforcement (an electric shock) to prevent him from making more. It seems like distant times and instead many of us grew up like this: with rewards and punishments , with sweets and punishments. In my work as an educator I see that educational systems based on conditioning and power still persist, where there are those who win and those who lose, those who command and those who execute, those who impose and those who obey and when this does not happen because the children, pupils, young people do not respond as we would like, educators are attacked by a sense of anger of sorrow and impotence.

The greatest power we can have is certainly not over others, but over us, and this is the great lesson that empathy-based pedagogy gives us every day. Hence, educating with empathy means profound respect for one's feelings , whether large or small, it means listening to the meaning that each of us attributes to our internal world, it is having faith in the human skills and qualities that are within us, as a sprout from birth.

Stop and observe

When the behavior of children and young people seems incomprehensible to our eyes, that is the moment to stop and observe, to listen without judging, leaving yourself the possibility of not knowing and not jumping to hasty conclusions, because every person always has a valid reason to express his no and his disagreements.

The child is not an empty container because already in prenatal life he lives immersed in his fertile environment and, subsequently, his growth will be guaranteed by an environment that facilitates his emotional, physical and spiritual development and will be that secure base, as John Bowly would say (1988), who will create the bonds that are the foundation from which we start to face our whole life and which will allow him to bear fruit in all his skills. Educating with empathy means entering into a relationship with our children , it means enriching ourselves by listening to another human being who has come to tell us something, look, there is another life, live better.

It means trying to put yourself in his shoes to feel how he feels, to see how he sees and to observe how the world looks to him. It means overcoming the concept that educating means putting something inside, but changing perspective and listening to what the child has inside him, to promote a climate that makes it easier for him to bring out his full potential.

Parents don't "teach" their children self-esteem, they transmit it to them first of all with their example, acting as a secure base from which to explore the world, and being a model of love and respect for themselves and for others.

We develop a sense of ourselves first of all starting from the significant relationships of childhood: as soon as the child is born, he has no self-awareness, but perceives the atmosphere of love that surrounds him. Parents are the mirror of his value and kindness and in their eyes, full of tenderness for him and admiration for his conquests, he catches that "sparkle" that sends back to him the sense of his being special , unique, loved by someone for he is so important, on whom his life depends and whom he perceives as omnipotent.

At the beginning of life , the sense of self is limited to physicality : it is on this terrain that the little ones begin to get to know each other, experience their ability to act on the world, through a rudimentary sense of mastery , lived in "society" with their parents , in the sense that they guarantee it. The ability to arouse the interest of those who look after him, to communicate with him, getting what he needs, is the basis of trust in himself and in others.

As he grows up, the disinterested affection of his parents, their acceptance of his limits, confidence in his ability to overcome them, respect for his needs, are the model of self-love which, internalized, forms the basis of future self-esteem . A child treated with coldness or hostility , open or hidden, or even adored , but for what he represents to the parent, not for who he is, not recognized in his needs of him, will develop a lack of self-esteem and, often, problems psychological and behavioral.

In the preschool age , the child has acquired some important certainties : his body belongs to him, he perceives himself as a thinking being, he is able to stay away from his parents and learns to deal with others. Self-descriptions still revolve around concrete characteristics (physical appearance, possessions owned by him), but he begins to glimpse the underlying psychological plane. Every day is a discovery , a new learning, and if there is a serene and encouraging climate around him, the little one will develop his potential in the best way.

The development of confidence and courage begins in early childhood and continues throughout the teenage years and into adulthood. These qualities are not innate, but rather they are learned and developed through a variety of experiences and influences.

As parents, it is our job to create an environment that fosters the development of confidence and courage in our children. This includes providing opportunities for them to learn and grow, setting clear boundaries and expectations, and encouraging them to take risks and try new things.

In short, confidence and courage are critical qualities that help children develop a sense of self-worth, resilience, and determination. By nurturing these qualities in your children, you can help them become confident and courageous adults who are prepared to face the challenges of life with grace and determination.

There are many ways that parents can help their children develop confidence and courage. Some strategies include:

- Providing positive reinforcement and

encouragement: Children need to feel supported and valued in order to develop confidence. By offering words of encouragement and praising your child for their efforts and achievements, you can help boost their self-esteem and build their confidence.

- Allowing children to make their own decisions: Giving children the opportunity to make their own choices and decisions, within appropriate limits, can help them develop confidence in their own judgment and decision-making skills.

- Encouraging children to try new things: By encouraging children to take on new challenges and experiences, you can help them develop the courage to step out of their comfort zone and try new things.

- Teaching children to problem-solve: By helping children learn to think through problems and come up with solutions, you can teach them to be confident and resourceful in the face of challenges.

- Modeling confidence and courage yourself: As a parent, you are a role model for your children. By demonstrating confidence and courage in your own actions and decisions, you can help your children learn to embrace these qualities as well.

- Teaching children to set and achieve goals: By helping children set and work towards specific goals, you can teach them the value of perseverance and help them develop the confidence to pursue their dreams.

- Encouraging children to express themselves: Allowing children to express themselves through art, music, writing, or other forms of self-expression can help them build self-confidence and courage.

- Helping children develop social skills: By teaching children how to communicate effectively, make friends, and navigate social situations, you can help them build confidence and courage in their interactions with others.

- Encouraging children to be physically active: Physical activity can help children build confidence and courage by teaching them to push their physical limits and face challenges head-on.

- Helping children develop coping strategies: By teaching children how to cope with negative emotions and stress, you can help them develop the resilience and courage they need to face challenges and overcome adversity.

By implementing these strategies, parents can help their children develop the confidence and courage they need to thrive in life. Remember to always be patient and supportive as your child grows and develops, and to offer encouragement and praise for their efforts and achievements. With a little guidance and support, your child can grow into a confident and courageous adult who is prepared to tackle any challenge that comes their way.

Ultimately, the key to nurturing confidence and courage in children is to provide a supportive and encouraging environment that fosters their growth and development. With patience, encouragement, and a willingness to help your children learn and grow, you can help your children become confident and courageous adults who are prepared to tackle any challenge that comes their way.

CHAPTER 2

Creating a Supportive and Encouraging Home Environment.

Creating a supportive and encouraging home environment is an important factor in helping children and adults thrive and achieve their full potential.

Creating a supportive and encouraging home environment is essential for the overall well-being and development of children. It is a space where children feel safe, loved, and valued, and where they can freely express themselves without fear of judgment or criticism.

The word environment can be misleading and suggest that it is a physical place, but it is only a partial interpretation of the term.
In fact , it is also and above all necessary that the human and cultural environment be favorable to learning .

What aspects to keep in mind to create a stimulating environment?

First of all, the relationship that underlies any learning.

A stimulating relationship is made of empathy, availability, encouragement, positivity.

An environment free from judgments and accommodating, without tension, stress, set goals and parental expectations is the condition for the child to feel welcomed for what he is and without the suspicion of having to adapt.

It is in this environment that the child feels able to move freely , to face the fatigue of investigation and exploration, to be able to risk making a mistake or making a fool of himself.

Within a non-judgmental relationship, the child also develops his own social skills, trains himself to be a person who knows how to listen and manages to put his talents to good use.

Here are a few ways to create a supportive and encouraging home environment:

- Provide a safe and comfortable space: Make sure your home is a place where your family feels physically and emotionally safe. This includes keeping your home clean and well-maintained, and creating a peaceful atmosphere.

- Encourage open communication: Encourage your family members to talk about their feelings, concerns, and goals. Creating an open and non-judgmental space for communication can help everyone feel heard and supported.

- Practice positive reinforcement: Rather than criticizing or punishing negative behavior, focus on praising and reinforcing positive behavior.

This helps to build confidence and self-esteem.

- Encourage independence: Encourage your family members to take on responsibilities and make their own decisions, within reason. This helps to build confidence and self-esteem.

- Set clear expectations and boundaries: Establishing clear expectations and boundaries can help to create a sense of stability and structure in the home. This can also help

children and adults feel more
secure and supported.

- Offer support and
  encouragement: Show your
  family members that you believe
  in them and are there to support
  them. Encourage them to
  pursue their goals and dreams,
  and offer help and guidance
  when needed.

- Foster a sense of community:
  Encourage your family members
  to get involved in their
  community, whether through
  volunteering, participating in
  local events, or simply getting to

know their neighbors. This can
help to create a sense of
belonging and connection.

Overall, creating a supportive and
encouraging home environment is all
about fostering a sense of love,
acceptance, and belonging for all
individuals within the household. By
focusing on positive reinforcement,
open communication, and a healthy
lifestyle, you can create a space where
individuals feel supported and
encouraged to grow and thrive.

CHAPTER 3

Teaching Your Child to Take Risks and Try New Things.

Encouraging your child to take risks and try new things can be an important part of their development and can help them learn and grow.

Teaching your child to take risks and try new things is an important part of their development and can help them grow and learn. It's natural for parents to want to protect their children and keep them safe, but it's also important to encourage them to step out of their comfort zone and try new things.

Here are some tips for teaching your child to take risks and try new things:

- Model risk-taking behavior: Children often look to their parents and other adults as role models, so it's important to show your child that you're willing to take risks and try new things yourself. This can help your child see that it's okay to take risks and try new things.

- Encourage independence: Help your child develop their own

interests and passions by giving
them the freedom to make their
own decisions and try new
things on their own. This can
help them develop confidence
and self-reliance.

- Provide a safe environment: It's
important to create an
environment where your child
feels safe and supported when
trying new things. This can
involve providing appropriate
supervision and support, as well
as being there to encourage and
motivate your child.

- Encourage a growth mindset: Help your child develop a growth mindset by praising their effort and persistence, rather than their innate abilities. This can help them see that they can learn and improve through hard work and practice, which can make them more willing to try new things.

- Encourage trying new things: Encourage your child to try new activities, hobbies, and experiences, and encourage them to take risks and try new things. This can help them develop a sense of adventure and curiosity, and can help them learn and grow in new ways.

- Gradually increase the level of risk: Start by encouraging your child to try small, low-risk activities, and gradually increase the level of risk as they become more comfortable and confident.

- Discuss potential risks and how to manage them: Talk to your child about the potential risks associated with trying new things and help them develop strategies for managing those risks.

- Celebrate their successes: When your child tries something new or takes a risk, be sure to celebrate their successes and accomplishments. This will help them feel proud of themselves and encourage them to continue taking risks and trying new things.

- Encourage a sense of adventure: Encourage your child to be curious and to explore the world around them. This can involve trying new foods, activities, or hobbies, and can help your child learn to be open to new experiences.

- Encourage teamwork and collaboration: Working with others can help your child learn to take risks and try new things in a supportive and collaborative environment. Encourage your child to join a team or club, or to participate in group activities that involve taking on new challenges.

- Encourage creativity and problem-solving: Encourage your child to think creatively and to come up with solutions to problems they encounter. This can help them learn to take risks and try new things in a safe and supportive environment.

Overall, the key to helping your child learn to take risks and try new things is to offer support, encouragement, and a safe and supportive environment. By doing so, you can help your child develop the confidence and resilience they need to take on new challenges and grow as an individual.

Remember, it's important to balance the need for safety with the need for growth and development. Encourage your child to take appropriate risks and try new things, but also make sure they have the support and guidance they need to stay safe.

CHAPTER 4

Helping Your Child Develop a Growth Mindset

A growth mindset is the belief that one's abilities and intelligence can be developed through effort and learning. This mindset is important for children because it can help them persevere in the face of challenges and setbacks, and it can also help them feel more motivated and confident in their abilities. Here are some tips for helping your child develop a growth mindset:

- Encourage effort and learning: Help your child understand that effort and learning are key to improving their skills and abilities. Encourage them to try new things and to work hard, even when they encounter challenges.

- Praise effort, not ability: When praising your child, focus on their effort and hard work rather than their innate abilities. This will help them understand that their abilities are not fixed, and that they can improve through effort and learning.

- Encourage them to take on challenges: Encourage your child to take on challenges and to see mistakes and setbacks as opportunities to learn and grow. Help them understand that it's okay to make mistakes, and that everyone faces challenges from time to time.

- Encourage a positive attitude: Help your child develop a positive attitude towards learning and challenges. Encourage them to stay positive and to look for the silver lining in difficult situations.

- Help them set goals: Encourage your child to set goals for themselves, and help them break those goals down into small, achievable steps. This will help them see progress and feel a sense of accomplishment as they work towards their goals.

- Encourage persistence: Help your child understand that persistence is an important part of the learning process. Encourage them to stick with things, even when they are difficult, and to keep trying until they succeed.

- Help them learn from failure: When your child faces setbacks or failures, help them see those experiences as opportunities to learn and grow. Encourage them to reflect on what they learned from the experience and to think about how they can use that knowledge to do better in the future.

- Encourage them to seek help: Help your child understand that it's okay to ask for help when they need it. Encourage them to seek out additional resources or support when they are

struggling with a task or
concept.

- Encourage self-reflection: Help
  your child develop the habit of
  self-reflection by encouraging
  them to think about their
  learning and progress.
  Encourage them to ask
  themselves questions like "What
  did I learn today?" or "How can
  I improve?"

- Encourage a growth mindset in
  others: Help your child
  understand the importance of a
  growth mindset and encourage
  them to help others develop this

mindset as well. Encourage your child to be a positive influence on their peers and to help others see the value of effort and learning.

- Encourage a love of learning: Help your child see the joy and value in learning by encouraging them to pursue their interests and passions. Encourage them to try new things and to discover new subjects and activities that they enjoy.

Overall, the key to helping your child develop a growth mindset is to encourage effort, learning, and a positive attitude towards challenges. By doing so, you can help your child learn to persevere in the face of setbacks and to believe in their own ability to improve and grow.

CHAPTER 5

Fostering a Sense of Purpose and Meaning in Your Child's Life.

Fostering a sense of purpose and meaning in your child's life is an important part of their development and can help them feel motivated, engaged, and fulfilled. Here are some tips for helping your child find purpose and meaning in their life:

- Encourage their passions and interests: Help your child explore their passions and interests and encourage them to

pursue activities that are
meaningful and fulfilling to
them.

- Encourage service and giving
  back: Help your child
  understand the importance of
  giving back and encourage them
  to get involved in service
  projects and community service.

- Encourage them to set goals:
  Encourage your child to set
  goals for themselves and to
  work towards achieving those
  goals. This can help them feel a
  sense of purpose and
  accomplishment.

- Encourage independence and self-sufficiency: As your child grows, encourage them to take on responsibilities and to make their own decisions. This can help them develop a sense of purpose and a sense of control over their own lives.

- Encourage gratitude: Help your child develop an attitude of gratitude by encouraging them to focus on the positive aspects of their life and to appreciate the things they have.

- Encourage mindfulness: Help your child develop mindfulness by encouraging them to be present in the moment and to focus on their thoughts and feelings.

CHAPTER 6

Teaching Your Child to Communicate Effectively and Assertively.

Teaching your child to communicate effectively and assertively can help them to feel more confident and empowered in their relationships with others. Here are some tips for teaching your child these important skills:

- Encourage open and honest communication: Encourage your child to express their thoughts, feelings, and needs openly and honestly. This will help them to become more confident and assertive in their communication.

- Practice active listening: Help your child to develop good listening skills by encouraging them to pay attention to what others are saying and show that they are listening through eye contact, nodding, and asking questions.

- Use "I" statements: Encourage your child to use "I" statements when expressing their thoughts and feelings. This helps to avoid blame and defensiveness in communication.

- Practice assertiveness: Help your child to learn how to express their own needs and boundaries in a respectful and confident way. This may involve role-playing or other activities to practice assertive communication.

- Encourage problem-solving: Help your child to develop problem-solving skills by encouraging them to come up with solutions to conflicts or challenges they face. This can help them to become more confident and effective communicators.

By teaching your child these skills, you can help them to become more confident and assertive communicators, which will serve them well in their relationships with others.

CHAPTER 7

Raising a Resilient Child: Coping with Failure and Setbacks.

Raising a resilient child involves helping them to develop the skills and coping strategies necessary to handle failure and setbacks. Here are some tips for raising a resilient child:

- Encourage a growth mindset: Help your child to understand that their abilities and intelligence can be developed and improved through effort and learning. This can help them to be more resilient in the face of setbacks.

- Teach coping strategies: Help your child to develop coping strategies such as problem-solving, seeking support, and finding meaning in their experiences. These strategies can help them to navigate difficult situations and bounce back from setbacks.

- Encourage persistence: Help your child to understand that setbacks and failures are a normal part of life and that it's important to keep trying.

Encourage them to persevere and persist in the face of challenges.

- Model resilience: As a parent, it's important to model resilience for your child. Show them how you handle setbacks and failures in your own life, and encourage them to do the same.

- Offer support and encouragement: Provide support and encouragement to your child when they face setbacks. Help them to understand that it's okay to feel upset or disappointed, but that they can learn from their experiences and try again.

By teaching your child these skills and providing them with support and encouragement, you can help them to become more resilient in the face of challenges and setbacks.

CHAPTER 8

Teaching Your Child to Set and Achieve Goals.

Teaching your child to set and achieve goals is an important skill that can help them to feel more confident, motivated, and successful in their endeavors. Here are some tips for teaching your child to set and achieve goals:

- Encourage goal-setting: Help your child to identify what they want to achieve and to set specific, measurable, achievable, relevant, and time-bound

(SMART) goals. This can help them to stay focused and motivated.

- Help them develop a plan: Once your child has set a goal, help them to develop a plan for achieving it. This may involve breaking the goal down into smaller, more manageable steps and setting deadlines for each step.

- Encourage self-reflection: Help your child to reflect on their progress and to identify any challenges or obstacles they may be facing. This can help them to

stay on track and to make
adjustments as needed.

- Offer support and
  encouragement: Provide
  support and encouragement to
  your child as they work towards
  their goals. This can help to
  boost their confidence and
  motivation.

- Celebrate successes: When your
  child reaches a goal, be sure to
  celebrate their accomplishment.
  This can help to reinforce the
  importance of setting and
  achieving goals and to build
  their self-esteem.

By teaching your child these skills, you can help them to become more motivated, confident, and successful in their endeavors.

CHAPTER 9

Encouraging Your Child to Be Independent and Self-Sufficient.

- Encourage your child to take on small tasks and responsibilities around the house, such as setting the table, putting away their own laundry, or helping with grocery shopping. This can help them develop a sense of ownership and independence.

- Encourage your child to make their own decisions and solve their own problems. This can help them develop critical thinking skills and confidence in their own abilities.

- Encourage your child to try new things and take on new challenges. This can help them develop resilience and a growth mindset.

- Encourage your child to express their own opinions and ideas, and listen to what they have to say. This can help them develop self-esteem and confidence in their own thoughts and ideas.

- Encourage your child to spend time on their own, either by giving them solo playtime or encouraging them to pursue interests on their own. This can help them develop independence and self-sufficiency.

- Encourage your child to take risks and try new things, even if they are afraid. This can help them develop courage and resilience.

- Encourage your child to be responsible and accountable for their own actions. This can help them develop a sense of ownership and self-discipline.

- Encourage your child to be independent and self-sufficient by setting clear expectations and boundaries, and allowing them to make their own mistakes. This can help them learn from their experiences and develop self-reliance.

CHAPTER 10

Teaching Your Child to Be a Good Friend and Teammate.

Teaching your child to be a good friend and teammate is an important part of their social and emotional development. Here are a few tips to help you get started:

- Lead by example: Children often learn by watching and imitating their parents and other adults. Show your child how to be a good friend and teammate by being kind, respectful, and supportive towards others.

- Encourage positive communication: Help your child learn to express themselves in a positive and respectful way. Encourage them to use "I" statements and to express their thoughts and feelings without blaming or judging others.

- Teach empathy: Help your child understand what others are feeling by encouraging them to put themselves in others' shoes. This can help them be more understanding and supportive towards their friends and teammates.

- Promote teamwork: Encourage your child to work together with their friends and teammates to achieve a common goal. This could involve sharing ideas, dividing tasks, and offering support and encouragement to one another.

- Encourage honesty and accountability: Help your child understand the importance of being honest and taking responsibility for their actions. Encourage them to be honest about their mistakes and to apologize when necessary.

By teaching your child these skills, you can help them develop strong friendships and become effective team players, which can benefit them both socially and academically.

CHAPTER 11

Helping Your Child Manage Emotions and Deal with Stress.

Helping your child manage emotions and deal with stress is an important part of parenting. Children may experience a wide range of emotions, including happiness, sadness, anger, fear, and frustration, and it's important to help them learn how to identify and cope with these emotions in healthy ways.

Emotional intelligence is the ability to recognize, understand, and manage one's own emotions, as well as the emotions of others. It's an important skill that can help children navigate social situations, form healthy relationships, and cope with stress.

Helping your child develop emotional intelligence can be a lifelong process, but it's an important investment in their overall well-being and success. By supporting your child's emotional development, you can help them learn to manage their emotions and navigate challenges with greater ease and resilience.

Here are some tips for helping your child manage emotions and deal with stress:

- Encourage your child to express their emotions: Help your child identify and name their emotions, and encourage them to talk about how they feel. This can help your child understand and manage their emotions better.

- Help your child practice relaxation techniques: There are many relaxation techniques that can help children cope with stress and manage their emotions, such as deep breathing, progressive muscle relaxation, and visualization. Encourage your child to try these techniques when they are feeling overwhelmed or stressed.

- Model healthy coping strategies: Children learn by example, so it's important to model healthy coping strategies for your child. This means taking care of your own emotional well-being and showing your child how to deal with stress and emotions in a healthy way.

- Set limits and establish rules: Establishing clear limits and rules can help your child feel more secure and in control, which can reduce stress and improve emotional regulation.

- Encourage physical activity: Physical activity can help children cope with stress and improve their emotional well-being.

Encourage your child to participate in activities they enjoy, such as sports, dance, or martial arts.

- Help your child develop problem-solving skills: Teaching your child how to identify and solve problems can help them feel more in control and better equipped to handle stress. Encourage your child to come up with solutions to challenges they face, and offer guidance and support as needed.

- Encourage healthy habits: Helping your child develop healthy habits, such as getting enough sleep, eating a balanced diet, and staying hydrated, can also improve their emotional well-being and help them cope with stress.

Remember, it's normal for children to experience a wide range of emotions and to feel stressed at times. By helping your child learn healthy coping strategies and supporting them as they learn to manage their emotions and deal with stress, you can foster their emotional well-being and set them up for success in the long run.

CHAPTER 12

Parenting for Confidence and Courage: A Summary and Reflection.

Parenting for confidence and courage involves teaching and modeling these important character traits to children. It involves helping children develop a sense of self-worth and the resilience to face challenges and failures.

Parenting is a challenging yet rewarding journey that involves helping our children grow into confident and courageous individuals. It is important to create an environment in which children feel safe to explore, take risks, and make mistakes. This can be achieved through a variety of approaches, including setting clear boundaries, modeling positive behavior, and encouraging independence.

One way to foster confidence and courage in children is by providing a supportive and nurturing environment. This can involve praising children for their efforts and accomplishments, rather than just their outcomes. It can also involve setting realistic expectations and providing opportunities for children to take on age-appropriate challenges and responsibilities.

Another way to promote confidence and courage in children is by teaching problem-solving skills. This can involve helping children identify and overcome obstacles, and encouraging them to think creatively and try new things.

It is also important to foster confidence and courage in children by providing them with opportunities to learn and grow. This can involve encouraging them to try new activities, providing them with resources and support to explore their interests, and giving them the freedom to make their own decisions and mistakes. It can also involve setting high expectations for their behavior and performance, and helping them to develop a strong work ethic.

Also important to model confidence and courage in your own behavior. Children learn by observing and imitating the adults around them, so it's important to show them how to handle challenges and setbacks with grace and determination.

Ultimately, parenting for confidence and courage involves helping children to develop the skills and attitudes they need to become confident and courageous adults. It involves helping them to find their passions and pursue their dreams, and supporting them as they navigate the challenges and setbacks that are a natural part of life. Through this process, parents can help their children grow into strong, capable, and resilient individuals who are able to face the world with confidence and courage.

Parenting for confidence and courage requires a combination of setting clear boundaries, providing positive reinforcement, fostering a growth mindset, and being supportive and encouraging. By focusing on these areas, parents can help their children grow into confident and courageous individuals who are prepared to tackle the challenges of life. So, parenting is not an easy task, but it is a very important and rewarding one.

Printed in Great Britain
by Amazon

39223936R00056